D1295057

SOUTH AFRICAN

ANIMAL ADVENTURES

JAY HEALE

CONTENTS

Just Nuisance 4

The Friendly Leopard 8

Hatsi the Dassie 12

Haig and Dimple 16

Adam the Elephant 20

Jack the Signalman 24

Jock of the Bushveld 28

Huberta the Hippo 32

The Famous Somerset 36

Smurf and Henry 40

The Fish with Four Legs 44

INTRODUCTION

Once there was a storyteller who, pipe in hand, searched his memory for long-gone adventures. Some stories he had told his young listeners before. They remembered them so vividly that at one point a hand was laid on his shoulder and a voice said, "Dad! You have left out the best part of all. Don't you remember how ..."

The storyteller decided to put that story down in writing. While he was busy doing so, his children urged him, "It must *all* be true! Don't leave out *anything*!"

That is how *Jock of the Bushveld* came to be written and according to Jock's owner, Sir Percy FitzPatrick, it is a true story from beginning to end.

So are all the stories in this book. All happened right here in South Africa. Some animals were wild and others tame, some famous and others little known. As strong bonds often develop between humans and animals, some of the stories are obviously about humans as well.

While I compiled this book, I took great care to check the facts of these tales, and I have made guesses only where the answer seemed fairly logical. In a few places I have guessed at the actual words of conversations, but storytellers are allowed to do that!

Some of these animals have already appeared in other books.
If you want to read these longer stories, ask your librarian for:

Jock of the Bushveld by Sir Percy FitzPatrick
Just Nuisance AB by Terence Sisson
Huberta's Journey by Cicely van Straten
Old Fourlegs by Prof JLB Smith
The Elephants of Knysna by Nick Carter
They Came From The Sea by Muriel Rowe

Just Nuisance

Many naval ships have had animal mascots – and many army regiments as well – but none have gained the same fame and popular affection as the Great Dane which was enlisted as a member of the Royal Navy just before the outbreak of the Second World War.

The puppy, bought by Benjamin Chaney in March 1938, was hardly a year old and it was already clear that he was going to grow into a large dog. When Benjamin and his wife were put in charge of the United Services Institute at Simon's Town, they took the young dog along. Most of their customers were naval ratings, wearing bell-bottomed dark blue trousers, the well-known three-striped collar and flat-topped seaman's cap. These were the humans who became the Great Dane's friends. Officers he tolerated and women he ignored!

It was just as well for the Chaneys' food bill that their dog enjoyed the company of the navy. A whole can of corned beef was merely a snack for him! Before long, at least one naval steward was craftily filling out his monthly return to include large amounts of canned corned beef which, when opened, "proved to have meat unfit for human consumption". These had been disposed of – in Nuisance's direction!

This name was swiftly awarded when the crew of HMS *Neptune* found they had to step around the huge dog's body as he sunned himself on one of their gangways. "You ... nuisance!" they complained – and the name stuck.

Simon's Town offered very little in the way of entertainment, so when the naval ratings were granted leave, they would board the train to Cape Town. Nuisance decided to go with his friends, but without a ticket. If a brave ticket-collector managed to persuade Nuisance to leave, he would either climb aboard again through the nearest open window or sit down on the platform and wait for the next train. The South African Railways authorities became increasingly annoyed and eventually threatened Chaney that the dog would be destroyed if it continued travelling without a ticket.

Messages were rushed around Simon's Town. How dare anyone threaten their huge pet? The Commander-in-Chief South Atlantic found himself swamped with letters of protest. So the decision was made. The dog Nuisance was to be officially enlisted as a member of the Royal Navy. That way the Admiralty could issue him with a season ticket.

On 25 August 1939, Nuisance entered the recruiting office of HMS *Afrikander I* for his papers to be registered. His trade was described as 'Bonecrusher' and his religion as'Scrounger'. No one knew what to put as his Christian name until someone suggested,

"Leave it out and give the name as just Nuisance." So the brainwave was accepted! And Able Seaman Just Nuisance was enroled in King George VI's Royal Navy. His name, rank and official number were fastened to his collar.

Just Nuisance was also supplied with a regulation seaman's cap. The strap under his chin annoyed him. He even gave a sigh when it was taken off at night. In due course he was given official authority to be the only member of the Royal Navy to be excused from wearing a seaman's cap.

He was billeted in Hut Number One where he had a bed of his own, took his meals at the same time as the other ratings, and was given shore leave every night. Corned beef and lamb chops were his favourite foods, followed by milk chocolate and ice cream. To drink he liked lager beer. Buying Nuisance a drink became so popular that a special notice had to be posted requesting all canteens and bars in Simon's Town not to serve him more than his nightly ration of six quarts (about 14 cans).

Though Just Nuisance had no official duties, he still contributed vigorously to South Africa's war effort by attending charity gatherings to raise money. In August 1941, he was 'married' to a Great Dane bitch named Adinda. When the resulting two puppies were old enough, they and Just Nuisance were welcomed to Cape Town by the Mayor and Mayoress and cheering crowds. The pups were full of bounce, tails wagging, tongues hanging out. Just Nuisance sniffed at them and gave one growl which seemed to mean, "If you're my kids, then behave yourselves." They did! And the puppies were sold by auction to raise funds for the war. So, even Just Nuisance contributed to the war effort.

Many letters arrived requesting the presence of the popular Great Dane at local fêtes and functions. In that way, he helped to raise hundreds of pounds for war funds. However, he simply couldn't go everywhere he was invited. Letters were written in reply on his behalf. He turned down one invitation on the grounds that "My C.O. informs me that my appearance might result in a flood of applications for service with the Royal Navy". To another admirer who seemed to think he was a sheepdog, Just Nuisance replied, "I'm not a sheepdog, nor do I like sheep except as mutton."

Life at Simon's Town wasn't all hard work. One day, Just Nuisance was sun-bathing beside the open-air pool. A fat officer dived in with a whale-like splash, swam a length (with much puffing and panting) and hauled himself out. The Great Dane was lying slightly in his way, so the nasty officer put a foot under the dog's belly and tipped him into the pool.

Just Nuisance swam up to the surface and looked hard at the officer, who was laughing loudly. Then he swam to the side where two of his friends helped him out. He shook himself dry and watched as the officer, still chuckling, dived in again. When he climbed out, Just Nuisance was waiting.

The Great Dane leapt forward and thrust his fore paws into the fat officer's bulging belly. As the man toppled helplessly back into the water, Just Nuisance gave one ear-shattering bark of triumph.

Amid the howls of laughter from all the sailors around, the officer threatened serious punishments for all of them and particularly for Able Seaman Just Nuisance. But nothing further happened.

One officer's indignation was unimportant compared to the way he befriended the hundreds

The GREAT DANE is a massive and powerful dog, with a muscular, well-formed body and a long arched neck. Its coat is very short and smooth, and is usually gold or black, or even a combination of the two colours. Originally bred in Germany to hunt wild boar, the Great Dane, despite its size and appearance, is generally friendly and playful, but is a very good watchdog and only aggressive when it is threatened.

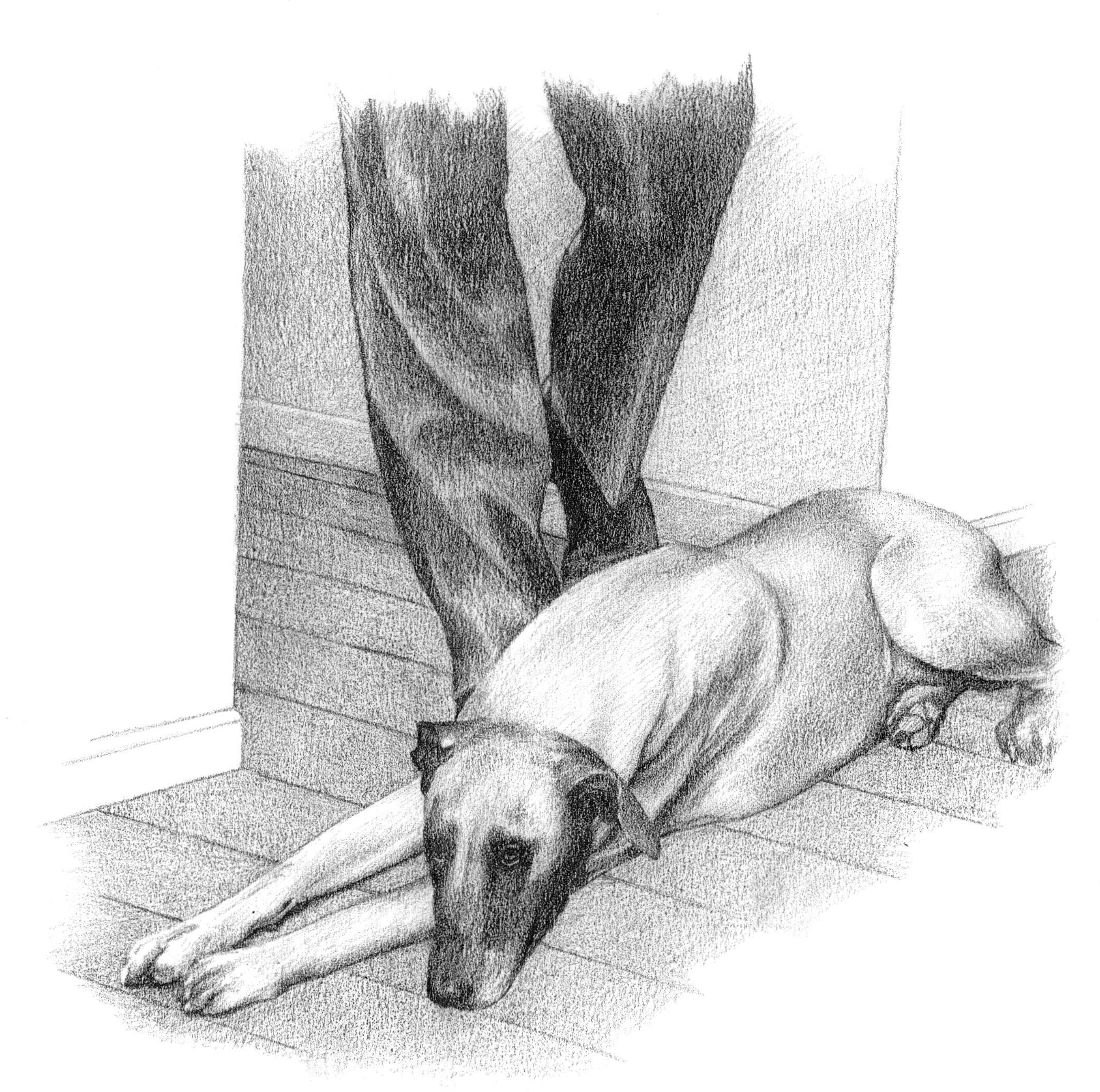

of ordinary seamen who visited Simon's Town. Just Nuisance knew nothing of the war these men were fighting. He knew only that they were honest workers who deserved his friendship.

Towards the end of 1943, it became clear that Just Nuisance was not well. He enjoyed riding in the naval transport lorries and often jumped off if he saw some of his friends walking past, and never bothered about how fast the lorry was moving. This had damaged his legs and now he was crippled with pain. For a few days he was given treatment at the naval hospital, where he lay stretched out sideways on a bed – with a bottle of lager beer as medicine on the bedside cupboard! He appeared to improve and was discharged as "fit for duty".

A month later he was very ill. A kind vet offered to look after him at his own home, but it soon became clear that Just Nuisance was in constant pain and that there was no chance of his recovery. Sorrowfully, the decision was taken that he should be put quietly to sleep. This was done on 1 April 1944 – his seventh birthday.

All available officers and men attended the funeral, and there were few dry eyes among them. Wrapped in the White Ensign, the body of Just Nuisance was buried with full naval honours. A party of Royal Marines fired the last volleys over the grave.

THE FRIENDLY LEOPARD

He lay in the bushes and watched the fishermen. He had seen them often before. These human beings didn't appear to be dangerous, though sometimes they made loud noises and played with fire. Since he left his mother to hunt on his own, the young leopard had kept out of sight of human beings. But now they were between him and the river. It had been a hot day and he was thirsty.

The leopard decided to go past them and down to the river. So he padded out from his hiding place, his paws making no sound on the dirt road.

But soon there was plenty of noise! Shrieks and yells, and running feet and car doors slamming, and engines starting up and bakkies driving away. People fell over each other and piled into the cars, whether the cars belonged to them or not!

That was a Saturday in mid-December, 1986 – and the story of the Betty's Bay leopard had begun.

About a week after the fishermen had encountered the leopard on the beach, the leopard padded its way into a braai area nearby. Again, there was a moment of panic as the humans rushed into the sea for safety. But then one girl darted back to fetch her camera and the leopard didn't seem to mind at all. She walked to within ten metres of the animal and took several photographs, while he sat there like a tame fireside cat. Already, his reputation as 'the friendly leopard' was growing.

But there was nothing friendly about the leopard when he discovered a breeding colony of jackass penguins in the reserve at Stony Point. Leopards kill to eat, by instinct. They often store the carcass of a large animal in a tree and return to it as a 'food store'. Perhaps sensing that one penguin was not a full meal, the leopard attacked the defenceless, waddling birds and in two nights he killed about 50

of them. From his point of view, the penguins were an easy source of food, but local opinion about the leopard suddenly changed from an amusing curiosity to a threatening and dangerous killer.

Concerned residents of Betty's Bay contacted biologist Peter Norton of the Cape Department of Nature and Environmental Conservation. He had made a special study of leopards in the Cape, so he went to investigate.

Concerned people had started to gather the pathetic bodies of the penguins. On the dead birds were tooth marks – certainly those of some large predator, either a lynx or leopard. And there was plenty of leopard spoor on the sandy patches around the reserve.

On a path were several tracks showing that the leopard came that way often, and Peter and his helpers started positioning a trap. It was a heavy cage with a steel frame and wire mesh. Hauling it into position was a rowdy affair. Suddenly one of the men pointed to behind Peter's back. Curious at the noise, the leopard had come to investigate. It was sitting watching them.

In the glowing light of the setting sun, the leopard looked even more golden. Peter Norton was very excited and quickly fetched his equipment from the bakkie. He couldn't waste the opportunity to shoot the leopard several times – with his camera. Lying relaxed on a rock, it gazed at him without seeming to be disturbed at all.

They set the trap and baited it with one of the dead penguins. As they retreated, the leopard strolled forward and sniffed at the cage. Cautiously, he pushed his head inside, seized the penguin and slid out without setting off the trap.

Peter then put another dead bird in the trap and, without hesitation, the leopard returned for a second helping. But this time he was too confident and the door snapped shut with a thud. He was caught.

After the widely reported killing of the penguins, such a swift capture of the 'murderer' made an excellent story for the newspapers and television. When Peter and his team returned to Stony Point the next morning, there were plenty of spectators, reporters and cameramen.

The Betty's Bay leopard was fast becoming famous.
The leopard lay relaxed in its cage, only objecting with a slight snarl when Peter approached and aimed his blowpipe. He blew the tranquillising dart into its rump. After some minutes, the leopard slumped as the powerful drug took effect.

The cage was opened and the beautiful spotted cat taken out. Working swiftly, Peter weighed and measured the animal. It was a male, about one to two years old, not yet grown to full size. Not much bigger than Peter's own golden retriever dog – but a lot more powerful. Around the leopard's neck he fastened a tough green collar with a radio device which would enable them to trace the leopard's movements.

"Where are you taking him?" asked one of the curious spectators.

"I can't tell you exactly," said Peter. "But it's somewhere out of harm's way in the mountains."

"He's beautiful!" murmured a boy, stroking the unconscious leopard.

"Nasty, dangerous thing," grumbled an adult nearby. "I'm glad to see the last of him."

The cage was placed in some high grass near a mountain stream in the heart of the Kogelberg Reserve. The door was opened and the leopard, sniffing the air, slid out to freedom.

The LEOPARD has a heavier head than the cheetah, and has rosettes of dark markings rather than spots like the cheetah. The leopard also has no dark 'tear lines' on its face. Normally, leopards hunt alone and at night and seldom allow themselves to be seen by man.

Leopards eat a wide variety of prey: mice, small antelope, birds and even river fish. A leopard does not roar like a lion: it gives a rasping cough or a growl.

Peter scratched his beard and wished the leopard good luck. But the leopard had other ideas.

In the warmth of a festive Saturday evening, just after Christmas, a young lady jumped into her car and, for a short distance, her fluffy miniature poodle ran playfully along behind.

Suddenly, out of the bushes appeared a slim yellow shape, speckled with black. The dog gave one frantic bark before the powerful jaws seized it and the leopard disappeared into the undergrowth. The news spread through the little town at once.

"The leopard is back!"

But there was no evidence that it was the Betty's Bay leopard. Peter Norton was fairly certain that it was *not*. Using the radio-collar, he had traced the leopard's movements for several days and 'his' leopard had been heading straight back towards the coastal region where he had been captured. That was expected, and Peter deliberately kept the press informed. The more the public knew about the habits and behaviour of leopards, the better. Following the radio signals from an aeroplane, Peter discovered that the leopard was now in the Botanical Gardens at Betty's Bay. By the time he had landed the plane and driven to the Gardens, he was met by three very disturbed gardeners. The leopard certainly *was* there!

"It jumped out of the bushes right in front of us. Made our hair stand on end! Then it bounded away into the garden."

So, while a television cameraman filmed the action from a cautious distance, Peter searched the bushes. Just before dark he managed to lure the leopard into the open to have his photograph taken again, before he slipped away.

Opinions of the residents were divided.

"It's a dangerous wild animal, I'm telling you, man."

"Nonsense! It's tame. It's our friendly leopard. It sat and looked at me like a puppy dog."

"If you leave it alone, it won't harm anybody."

Stories of hunters following wounded leopards have given them the reputation of savage behaviour, but this one was different. Most leopards living near civilisation hunt only at night because they are scared of humans. This one was unafraid of humans and seemed almost intrigued by them.

The next day Peter once again went in search of the leopard. He knew that if he could get the leopard and the photographer together, he had a unique opportunity to prove to television-watchers that wild animals did not need to be shot on sight.

Peter explained. "All wild animals *can* be unpredictable, but very few are naturally aggressive. You respect wild animals and they'll respect you. The very worst thing to do is to start screaming!"

So, while the fascinated cameraman followed and filmed every move, Peter and the leopard played 'cat and mouse' with each other. The leopard would hide and Peter would creep up close; then Peter would walk away and the leopard would trail him; then Peter hid and the leopard set out to find him. Not wishing to give the leopard a fright, Peter rose slowly from behind his bush. For a moment the two faces gazed at each other, one whiskered and one bearded, until the leopard strolled away. This leopard certainly was friendly.

Peter Norton knew that, for the leopard's own safety, he would have to be moved to a reserve such as the one at Cape Point from which he could not escape. It would be only a matter of days before the leopard could be moved to safety.

But then Peter received a phone call from a farmer in Pringle Bay. He had seen a leopard near his grazing sheep. Peter drove out to the farmer's smallholding, but it was already too late. In the back of the farm bakkie lay the body of the leopard. The once glowing yellow eyes were now dull, and green flies were buzzing around them.

The bullet that killed this beautiful animal was just one more shot fired in the battle between farmers and wildlife. In its short life, this leopard had captured the public's attention and so made its own tremendous contribution to their awareness of the problem. There *are* still wild animals in Africa.
It is the humans
who need to live
and let live.

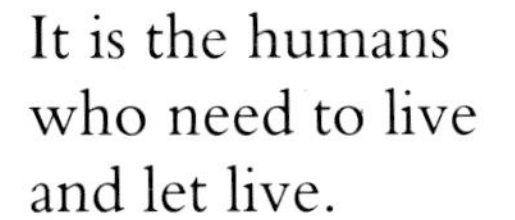

HATSI THE DASSIE

It was Christmas and the house was decorated with paper chains, strings of tinsel and a real Christmas tree with balls and baubles and chocolate bells wrapped in silver foil. At least that is what it looked like at night, when Susan and Steven went to bed.

In the morning, all the decorations were tattered and chewed, several chocolate bells were missing, and the presents under the tree showed clear teeth marks. Christmas was certainly not the right time of year to welcome a mischievous, little orphan dassie into the house!

"It's fun," said Susan, trying to convince herself.

"It's monstrous," said Steven and he meant it.

What was more, there were two of them. Two sweet, furry, young dassies, each about the size of a rat with no tail. They had fat cheeks, black button noses and nibbled with two flat, plastic-looking teeth on the top and a row of tiny teeth on the bottom. Both had pale eyebrows and their mouths had a permanent silly grin.

"They're so soft and friendly," said Susan protectively, as she stroked the soft brown hair on their round little tummies.

"Then why do they try to bite me?" asked Steven. "I only tried to stroke one, and he whirled around and threatened me!"

"That's because of their 'touch hairs'," explained Susan. "The hairs tell the dassie how close it is to things. Like an early-warning system."

Steven wasn't impressed.

All the books Susan had studied insisted that dassies are very lazy and do nothing for most of the day. Her two weren't like that at all. Like most small children, they were on the move all the time. They thought that good, healthy food was boring. They preferred to have a leisurely chew on more interesting items – preferably elastic or plastic or cotton wool.

They could climb just about anything. The pads on their feet actually sweat, which gives them enough grip to climb almost straight up steep cliffs. Their greatest game, apart from climbing the walls, was to jump on top of the kitchen dustbin which had a flip top. So they fell in. Then they squealed until Susan came to rescue them and put them on the floor, from where they could both jump back up again.

Susan and Steven did not agree about having dassies in the house, and they certainly could not agree on any names. 'Hansel and Gretel' was turned down flat – these were no fairy-tale characters! Susan wondered romantically about 'Romeo and Juliet'. Steven suggested 'Chew and Chomp' as being far more suitable. For the time being the two dassies had to be satisfied with plain 'He and She'.

But there weren't going to be two for much longer. She fell ill. She had an upset tummy and none of the cures that Susan tried had any effect. The vet felt her carefully and admitted that though dassies were not his usual patients, her insides didn't feel normal.

"Is it possible," asked the vet, "that she has eaten something harmful?"

Steven snorted. "Is there anything she hasn't eaten?"

"Then perhaps I'd better open her up and have a look. Bring her to my surgery tomorrow."

Susan stayed up all night with the suffering dassie, trying to encourage her to eat something. She needed food inside her for strength, as she hadn't eaten all day. She did nibble a little fish, which she had never touched before. Susan managed to get her to drink some medicine for her aching tummy. She chirruped with pleasure at the taste, and He promptly arrived to try some. Susan had to stop them arguing over it.

Poor She! Her tummy was so sore that she whistled faintly all the time. She didn't know whether to sit or stand or lie on the heating pad which Susan had provided as a bed. By morning, She seemed to have gained a little strength, but Susan was worried that it might not be enough.

The vet operated, but found nothing dangerous in her stomach, although he did notice that the stomach wall was thickened in some places and thin in others. But the shock of it all must have been too much for the little dassie, and She did not come round from the anaesthetic.

Left on his own, He was very sad and terribly alone. Steven tried to play with him, but the little dassie was not in a playful mood. He moped and whimpered, looking around nervously for his lost companion. Susan fetched her own precious teddy bear and

He snuggled up to it that night.

"Perhaps we're wrong to keep him," suggested Steven.

"Nonsense," said Susan. "He's unhappy. Wouldn't you be if I died? He needs company."

After a day of moping and another night with the teddy bear, the dassie suddenly cheered up and landed on the bed first thing in the morning. Having climbed all over Susan and Steven, he moved on to the bedside table and finished off the remains of last night's coffee from the bottom of the mugs.

"He likes mine better than yours," joked Steven.

"That's because you fill it with sugar," Susan decided. "He mustn't have too much. It'll be bad for his teeth."

"Hatsi Dassie!" said Steven, for no particular reason.

"Hatsi and teddy bear!"

"Hatsi-bear."

So that became He's new name. Hatsi decided that Susan was his new companion. He followed her everywhere. When Susan lay on her stomach on the floor – which was the position she liked best for reading – Hatsi would come running. He would first sniff her left ear to make sure it was the one he wanted, and then suck her earring with a soft but high-pitched squeal. Though Susan was expecting it, the noise always made her jump. When Hatsi had finished with her ear, he would gaze into space with his tongue out, sucking thoughtfully.

One day, the sitting room had been decorated for a children's party and there were balloons. Hatsi discovered that by standing on the back of the rocking-chair he could just reach one bunch. He stretched out and pulled. The bunch floated to the floor and Hatsi jumped off the chair quickly.

He sat beside the balloons and touched the first one carefully with his paws, feeling its shiny softness. It was twice his size. Then he discovered the knot and thoughtfully started to chew it. There was a loud pop (which must have been even louder for dassie ears) but Hatsi didn't flinch. He hesitated for a few seconds, obviously wondering if all balloons behaved like that, before he started on the next one. By the time Steven, shaking with laughter, had fetched Susan, the floor was covered with shreds of coloured rubber. Susan dashed to gather up the pieces.

"Hatsi might swallow some," she gasped.

"He probably has," was Steven's comment. "He's a plucky little fellow. I'm getting quite fond of him."

Hatsi chewed almost anything, but there was no doubt about what he wanted to eat: cereal, with milk, in different flavours. Hatsi would stand upright on his back feet, squealing, to indicate which flavour he had decided on. Oh, this stupid human! Why couldn't she understand? Susan would try a little of each until she found out what he was asking for. All biscuits were popular, however, and she had to hide the packets.

The sun shone in the late summer. There was nothing Hatsi-bear liked better than sun-bathing. He lay on his tummy with all four legs stretched out, drinking in the warmth from the stone stoep and the sun above.

Steven was busy, one day, scooping leaves out of the swimming pool with a long-handled net. Hatsi opened his eyes, blinked and saw something that interested him at the far side of the pool. He didn't appear to notice the large stretch of water in between. In mid run, he was suddenly treading on air and then splashed into the water. Steven forgot all about the net and jumped in, fully clothed. As he floated towards the surface, he could see the dassie above him, with all four feet paddling fiercely in the water.

"So dassies can swim," he observed, when he had hauled himself out and stood dripping by the pool with Hatsi unperturbed beside him. "There's more to this animal than I'd realised."

Though Steven was coming to like the furry, naughty Hatsi-bear dassie, Susan was growing desperate. She believed in discipline. Hatsi, however, had ideas of his own – and he loved Susan's sewing table with its treasure store of cotton reels, ribbons and bits of material.

"Off, off, off!" shouted Susan for the hundredth time as Hatsi jumped up.

The dassie scurried for cover behind a cushion until he thought Susan wasn't looking, and then jumped back again.

Susan sighed in loving despair, yet she was the one to object when Steven suggested that they take Hatsi with them on their coming holiday. A week at the coast, fishing and relaxing!

"We'll never relax with Hatsi there," she moaned.

"But we can't leave him behind," Steven pointed out. "None of our friends are crazy enough to want him. Anyway, I rather enjoy the little chap's company. Let's give him a holiday as well."

So Hatsi-bear found himself in a holiday cottage by the sea. His first discovery was that the back of the fridge was wonderfully warm, and far easier to get into than the one at home. He curled up and went to sleep, while Steven and Susan searched desperately for him.

Then he discovered the world outside! He hopped on to the windowsill and couldn't believe his eyes. All he could see was trees and sea and space – an open horizon stretching away for ever. Hatsi sat and gazed and looked and dreamed and dozed on that windowsill all day long.

He didn't want to go out and join the world he could see. In fact, when Susan took him outside, he ran back in again and returned to his perch on the windowsill. There was so much out there which needed considering.

When he wasn't gazing out of the window, or guzzling down milk and cereal, he was sitting quietly on the arm of Susan's chair, with a piece of cobweb on the end of his nose. He was facing Susan, but she knew from the glazed look in his eyes and the blank expression on his little face that he was almost asleep. The wide world outside had given him far too much to think about.

So together they sat and dreamed of more holidays by the sea.

The DASSIE or rock rabbit could well be the 'hyrax' mentioned in the Bible. Living in colonies amongst the rocks, the dassie is a sun-lover; he only emerges when the sun is up, enjoys sun-bathing, and goes to sleep before sunset. You can find dassies all over South Africa, but you should approach them carefully. A watchful male will bark to warn the others. They can also grunt, growl, wail, twitter and snort.

Haig and Dimple

There have been several Haigs and Dimples in the Port Elizabeth Oceanarium, but the original dolphins deserve their fame.

Let's go back to a morning in October 1962. A friendly traffic officer brought the news that dolphins had been sighted off Summerstrand beach. Swiftly, Colin and Muriel and the rest of the team from the Oceanarium were on their way in a Landrover with a boat on a trailer behind. As they went charging down the beach, the traffic officer joined them.

"I phoned my boss and asked for a day off!" he explained.

The outboard motor was started and the boat pulled away, trailing a long spread of netting. They circled the school of dolphins, but several made a break for it and avoided the net. The boat turned in towards the shore, pulling the net closer around two dolphins in shallower water. The dolphins seemed quite calm, while the 300 people gathering on the beach were in a frenzy of excitement! Colin and Muriel rushed into the water and eased the dolphins ashore as they tried to escape the net. It was important not to let their skins become dry, so the onlookers were urged to keep splashing water on the dolphins.

One at a time, the dolphins were lifted on to the Landrover – a process that needed at least a dozen strong men. Swathed in spare items of clothing, the first dolphin was quickly driven to the Oceanarium. More willing hands were waiting there to help carry the heavy dolphin to her new home in the large dolphin pool.

While the vehicle raced back to fetch the second dolphin, they watched their first guest, apparently quite at ease as she swam lazily amongst the other 2 500 fish in the main tank.

The second dolphin arrived, helped in by the off-duty traffic officer. It was only seven minutes since they had caught the pair on the beach. The team stood at the observation window of the tank and heard a noise like birds chirping. The dolphins were talking to each other!

As they watched, the smaller dolphin came close up underneath the larger one, nuzzled her snout in and began to suckle her mother's teats. So the dolphins were mother and daughter!

Now all they needed were names. They were bottlenose dolphins and, as someone seemed sure those must be whisky bottles, the two were duly named Haig and Dimple, after a very famous brand of whisky.

Then came the training. Muriel was soon balanced on a ladder, dangling a fish. Her eyes were on Dimple, as Haig (the younger one) seemed too shy. Suddenly, pain flashed through her arm – as if a donkey was trying to swing from her finger! The fish had been snatched by Haig, who had also bitten

Muriel's index finger down to the bone. Muriel yelled in pain and scolded the young dolphin – and within a few days both Haig and Dimple were taking fish from her hands without snatching.

Gradually the dolphins gained confidence and stayed closer to their human friends. When a fish was fixed on the end of a bamboo stick, Haig was quite used to jumping for her titbit.

"Local dolphin leaps to fame" said the local paper, and crowds started arriving for a 'show'. Large coloured beach balls were left in Haig's pool so she could play. She was becoming quite tame, and Muriel had sessions of 'talking' to her. Haig would turn over in the water for her tummy to be rubbed, often finishing by closing her eyes and sinking to the bottom in sheer ecstasy.

But nothing would persuade Dimple to jump.

Dimple also refused to eat. She stayed out in the middle of the tank, swimming slowly with eyes half-closed, sometimes with Haig supporting her. One morning she was found dead in her tank. An examination showed that she was just a very old dolphin. There was no sign of disease or injury, and her teeth were well worn down. She had died of old age.

However, it seemed wise to find a new companion for Haig. So, about a month after Dimple's death, the news that three Indian dolphins had been caught, was received with much jubilation. When they were all placed in the same tank, they swam happily together, and Haig even tried to flirt with one of them. But though the Indian dolphins leapt out of the water occasionally, they would not jump for fish the way that Haig did.

"Why does Haig have to jump for her food?" a visitor asked one day. "Isn't that rather cruel?"

"The dolphins are fed regularly," Muriel explained. "The jumps are just part of the show, for an extra snack! And it certainly isn't cruel. The louder you clap, the higher Haig jumps! She loves showing off"

It was Colin who became Haig's main trainer. He taught her to play with a ball, to bring back rubber rings and to balance a plastic telephone on her nose. For extra style, she 'wore' a pair of outsize sunglasses. She even learned to jump through a hoop. Her act usually ended with the command from Colin, "Wave goodbye nicely!" whereupon she went underwater and stuck her tail out, waving a sort of goodbye.

He also made many recordings of the whistles and sounds made by her. Most dolphin sounds come from the blowhole at the top of the head through which they breathe, or through their vocal chords which produce notes much higher than humans can make. Their level of intelligence is similar to that of a six-year-old child. Haig was certainly more intelligent than some humans. One of her visitors said he had come to see the mermaid!

However, there was one trick which Colin could not train Haig to perform properly. He had a small organ built with five keys, trying to train Haig to press the right notes with her snout to play a tune. But Haig preferred to play her own tune! She could also blow a hooter bulb and ring a bell.

Between performances, Haig would swim around watching the audience, first with one eye, then the other. Perhaps she thought they were let in to entertain her!

By the time Haig had been at the Oceanarium for a year, the Indian dolphins had died. Another Dimple had been found but she had died too. Haig's next companion was a dolphin called Lady. Though Haig accepted Lady, she occasionally pined for other company. Her health was not helped by the litter discarded into the main pool. Once, Haig was so ill that she brought up two handkerchiefs, six sucker sticks, a baby's dummy, a plastic bag, a headscarf and a piece of bamboo.

When John Haig and Company, the whisky producers, donated a large sum of money to help build a larger pool, it seemed only fair that Lady should be renamed Lady Dimple!

But both dolphins were soon pining for company, and became uninterested in food. They swam slowly, refusing to perform any tricks or leaps. The situation was desperate. Telephone calls were made to America to have a male dolphin flown over, but there were none to spare.

Thanks to the friendly whisky distillers, the Oceanarium was given a new and larger net. With this, in due course, two male dolphins were caught on the same day. As the first newcomer was being pushed gently into the tank, Haig spotted it and almost went mad. She swam around the tank like a ship's torpedo. When the second bull dolphin arrived, both Haig and Lady Dimple were clearly feeling better. As Colin and Muriel and the other Oceanarium staff celebrated the future, the two bulls were swimming contentedly in the middle of the tank while Haig and Lady Dimple performed a ballet dance of happiness around them.

Before long, Lady Dimple was seen to be pregnant. Telegrams of congratulation poured in from all over the country, and someone even put notices in the 'engagements' column of the Port Elizabeth newspaper.

And on that cheerful note, let us leave the happy dolphins!

The DOLPHINS which perform at the Port Elizabeth Oceanarium are bottlenose dolphins. Up to 4 metres long, they are black or dark grey with a white belly. Any dolphin you see close inshore in South African waters is likely to be of this type, or perhaps an Indian dolphin which is grey, with a curved dorsal fin.

Dolphins are extremely intelligent creatures. Their friendliness towards humans is proven by the news report that, after the floods in Bangladesh following a cyclone, a dolphin brought a human baby to the shore, carrying it gently on its snout.

ADAM THE ELEPHANT

There actually are elephants in the Knysna forests. You won't see them very often, because they are wise enough to keep away from the traffic on the national road. But just occasionally, in the very early morning, one elephant may stroll across the road.

Back in June 1970, the game warden who was studying and listing the Knysna elephants, woke to the sound of hammering on his caravan. No, it wasn't an elephant! It was one of his helpers, and he was very excited.

"Listen! There's an elephant in the Garden of Eden."

It sounded suitable. There probably were elephants in that biblical Garden. The warden dressed hurriedly, grabbed his camera, and the two of them drove through the grey of dawn towards the popular picnic spot on the N2 freeway. The occasional car whizzed past, ignoring the ancient forest on either side and what creatures might live there. They saw nothing.

Suddenly, there he was. He stood in the dark among the trees, like a statue. The warden watched the elephant with pleasure. Appearing in the Garden of Eden, he just had to be called Adam! He was exactly right in that forest setting. It was the cars and humans and noise and litter that were out of place.

The warden looked hopefully through the view-finder of his camera. There wasn't enough light yet for a photograph. Still, he had to try. Quietly, he walked down the road, leaving his helper with instructions to stop any traffic if he could. The elephant was in full view now, facing the road with the ferns and shrubs up to his belly. Both big tusks were plainly visible, the left one slightly curved.

Then Adam saw the approaching human. The trunk went up and an ominous rumble came from it as he blew what was clearly a warning.

At that moment, there was a lull in the traffic and absolute silence reigned. The elephant returned to what was obviously on his mind. Without hesitation, he moved forward and stepped swiftly across the road. He seemed aware of the traffic, and had waited for the right moment to cross. The warden lifted his camera as Adam approached the white line in the middle and snapped the trigger. Then the elephant disappeared among the green trees of the forest on the other side of the road.

With the help of skilled trackers, the warden searched later that morning, and found Adam deep in the heart of the forest. There was no point in disturbing him and he seemed contented on his own. There were other elephants in that area. Perhaps he was on his way to join them.

Three days later, the phone rang in the forester's office.

"A message from Knysna. The elephants have completely destroyed the new timberyard on the main road."

The game warden was soon in his car, wondering as he drove how the elephants had managed to 'destroy' the stores of indigenous timber and the expensive chain wire fence. Would some fool now go out after them with a rifle? He put his foot down and overtook lorries full of logs in the style of police cars in the best films.

The timberyard didn't seem destroyed at all when he arrived. The wooden buildings were intact; so were the piles of valuable timber. There was a gap in the fence nearest the forest, where the elephants had broken in. At the other end, apparently seeking the normal way out, the elephants had found the gates locked. So they had put their feet on the top bar and flattened both halves of the gate.

There was no indication why they had done this damage. An extra half minute's walk would have taken them around it. But elephants are stubborn about their right of way. One local farmer had a

rose garden near the forest, and the elephants frequently cut across one corner of it. They would carefully push down the fence, help themselves to a mouthful of rosebush or azalea, and go on their way.

There was little that the warden could do at the timberyard except make encouraging noises to the forester, and express confidence that "steps would be taken". (By whom, the warden had no idea!)

Having picked up Adam's spoor in the forest nearby, the warden took steps of a different kind. There might be the chance of a better photograph this time. The tracks led towards a shallow valley, with huge old oak trees, near the old road to Knysna. At one point, Adam had pulled a tree down and it landed halfway across the road. An early morning motorist had managed to swerve in time and brush past the top branches. The warden sighed. He knew that if the driver had driven carelessly or too fast and hit the tree, the popular outcry would have been against the elephant, not the bad driver.

The tracker led the game warden across the road to a plantation where Adam was quietly digging away at something in the ground. It was the first time the warden had ever seen an elephant among pine trees. He approached slowly, camera in hand, upwind and uphill. At last he was quite close and waited for Adam to lift his head so that his tusks would show clearly in the photograph.

Suddenly, to the warden's surprise and delight, a bushbuck stepped out of the high weeds and stood still, looking at him with what seemed mild astonishment.

This posed a problem. Of course, he wanted to get a shot of the bushbuck and the elephant together. As the warden stood rigid, for fear of scaring the buck, Adam raised his head. If the bushbuck was frightened by the click of the camera, would she dash off with her typical dog-like bark? And if so, would the elephant become more alert and annoyed? At last the picture was taken. Adam hadn't moved.

His arms were aching from holding the camera still so long. The warden lowered it and the bushbuck turned and trotted back into the shrubs. No bark, no sound at all.

He studied Adam through his binoculars. The elephant's tusks were long and yellow.

ELEPHANTS were once common in South Africa, but today you will find them only in the north of Zululand and the Transvaal lowveld, with a protected herd in the Addo Reserve and a small herd living wild in the ancient Knysna forests. There are, however, plans to introduce more elephants from the Kruger National Park into the Knysna forests so that the forest herds will increase.

The average height of an African elephant is 3,2 to 3,35 metres and a bull can weigh about six tons: he spends about 16 hours of each day eating and may consume up to 300 kilograms of food daily. Though the elephant walks about 10 kilometres per hour, it can charge at about 40 kilometres per hour when angered! Elephants live in herds, and mothers look after the calves for two years.

The tip of the left one was broken off. Most interesting was a hole in the top of his left ear: a neat round hole which could only have come from a bullet. So someone had taken a shot at him, probably some while before.

Adam's hump just brushed a trailing branch. The warden made a note of the tree and the next day, he measured the height. The elephant stood at 3,2 metres – no world record, but a fair-sized hunk of elephant by African standards.

He was certainly large enough to attract more photographers than merely the game warden. Some days later, two professional photographers arrived from Johannesburg to film the Knysna elephant. The warden agreed to help, but warned them that if Adam decided to charge, they must drop everything and run for their lives!

With the help of two trackers they managed to find Adam asleep under a tree. Their plan was simple. Pierre, with colour film in his camera, would move as close as possible with the warden, while Chris, with the camera with the black-and-white film, would photograph both of them and (hopefully) the elephant too.

Following a path through the forest, they all watched and listened carefully. The slightest noise might send the elephant either away from them or towards them! A glimpse of elephant hide showed in a shaft of sunlight peeping from between the leaves above.

The warden crept closer very quietly. He could see Adam's ears flapping against the afternoon heat. About 20 metres away, he stopped and examined the situation. By good fortune, Adam was facing in precisely the right direction. The first few paces he took would bring him on to the path, directly in view of the eager cameramen.

Back went the warden to where the photographers waited, loaded with heavy cameras and satchels of spare equipment. "Wait until he wakes up and steps out on to the path," he whispered. "But don't forget: if I say 'run', you run! Put your camera down if you have to. We can always fetch it later."

"I hope you're right," was the murmur from one of them.

Chris took up position on a high tree stump. Pierre and the warden moved ahead.

Adam had not moved. He stood there, swaying slightly. Pierre sighted his video camera and checked the focus. It seemed like years before Adam woke and decided to move.

There was no warning. There was Adam – much less than 25 metres away. Pierre pressed his button and a noise like a fairy football rattle came from his camera. It whirred remorselessly, and Adam swung to a halt, turned around and then charged towards them.

"Run!" urged the warden, and did so. Behind them came the rumbling thud of the elephant's feet. Ahead of them, Chris and the two trackers had disappeared into the forest.

They ran until they had no breath left in their lungs. Silence behind them. No elephant in sight. They paused for a cigarette and laughed together. Obviously, Adam had seen them retreat in such an undignified fashion, and was satisfied.

The next day they went back for the leather satchels full of equipment and spare reels of film. But Adam had found them and torn them to pieces. The camera was safe, though fragments of films and lenses were scattered far and wide.

"They seem to be such quiet creatures," said Chris to Pierre, thoughtfully.

"Now you know better," the warden advised them. "They are wild animals. And magnificent. May they stay with us a long time."

JACK THE SIGNALMAN

The door of the railway cottage opened and a brownish-grey baboon came out, hurried to the pump in the garden and worked vigorously at the handle, pumping water into a bucket. Then he carried the bucket inside. A while later, the baboon reappeared and went over to where a light trolley stood beside the railway track. He pushed the trolley up until its front wheels touched the rails, then he sat back on his haunches, threw the wheels over the rail, gave the whole thing a twist and a push, and the trolley was ready to roll along the track.

"All ready, Jack?" called a voice from the cottage. Out came a man in railway uniform and flat, peaked cap. He moved awkwardly as both his legs ended in wooden pegs. He sat himself down on the trolley, wooden legs poking out at the front.

"Oh, bother!" said the man. "I've forgotten my stick."

The baboon hurried back to the cottage, came out with the walking stick, locked the front door and brought both stick and key to his master. Then the baboon gripped the back of the trolley with his forepaws, pushed strongly with his back feet and so propelled the signalman along the line to his signalbox.

As James Edwin Wide travelled to work in this unusual fashion, he often thought back to that dreadful day in 1877 when he was helped out of Port Elizabeth hospital. He had been in despair. He had no faith in himself, few friends, and – worst of all – no legs. He had been a railway guard until a train had swept too close and knocked him down. All the railway officials could offer him at the time was the job of gatekeeper at a level crossing.

Moving about on his wooden legs to open gates and change the points had been so slow and painful that James had made himself this same light trolley which could run on the railway track. He had a big mongrel dog to pull the trolley, and found he could travel faster and easier that way. His confidence returned – and he was promoted to signalman at Uitenhage station.

That was when James saw a half-grown baboon for sale in the market near the station. The poor creature looked so forlorn that it reminded James of his own recent despair. He bought the baboon and named it Jack. It was the wisest thing James had ever done in his life. With a wide leather belt around its waist attached to a chain, Jack the baboon joined the dog in pulling the trolley along the rails. And when the dog was run over by a train, much the same way that James had been, Jack took over the trolley by himself. But there was one difference – he found it easier to push than to pull, so James took off Jack's chain and let him do just that. When they came to a downhill slope, Jack jumped joyously on the back of the trolley and the two of them skimmed along together!

One of James' duties as signalman was to take charge of the key of the padlock which locked points off the Graaff-Reinet line leading to the coal-yard. Puffing and blowing, the first morning train arrived, slowed down and gave the usual signal of four toots on the hooter to let James know that coal was wanted. Usually James hobbled into the signalbox, took the key from its nail on the wall, went out again and handed it to the driver as he steamed slowly past the platform.

But today Jack got there first. As soon as the four toots sounded, the baboon scampered inside, gripped with one hand on the top of the closed half-door to lift himself up, and grabbed the key with the other. Then he ran onto the platform and held out the key to the astonished train driver.

"That baboon your assistant, James?" he asked, laughing.

"Couldn't manage without him," answered James – and he knew that was the truth. "You're intelligent, aren't you, Jack? The best companion a man could have." He fondled the baboon tenderly and for a moment they seemed to cuddle each other. Jack knew his master was pleased, so he added this easy task to his other skills. From that day on, James never had to fetch the key again.

Of course, the main job of a signalman was to work the signals. Each lever in the signalbox was joined by a greased wire to its signal arm or junction point on the rails. It was hard work for a fit man; it was heavy work for a man with no legs. Even when no points had to be changed, there were 'distant' and 'home' signals to set for each train, and then they would have to be reset again afterwards.

After months of training the baboon, James knew that all he had to do was call out the name of the lever and Jack would instantly pull it. A whistle would be heard in the distance and Jack would spring to the correct 'home' signal while his master pulled on the heavier 'distant' signal lever. Once the train was past, Jack silently pushed his lever back into position and then chattered his delight as James patted him on the head.

"What's that flea-ridden ape doing in your signalbox?" rasped a voice from the doorway.

"He's helping with the signals," James explained mildly. "He's done it for months. I've been training him."

"Don't you dare do it again!" The burly foreman shook his fist at James. "I'll report you. I'll have you fired."

The threatening tone upset the baboon. He snarled, showing his heavy teeth, and ran at the foreman knocking him off balance.

"You hairy brute!" shouted the foreman. "I'll teach you!" But he was still on one leg as Jack charged him, shoulder to shoulder. The foreman staggered back and fell off the edge of the platform.

There were no trains near, but his dignity had been insulted. He seized a stick and climbed back onto the platform. As soon as he advanced on the baboon, Jack grabbed an empty coal sack and used it as a whip. Screaming with indignation, he beat the foreman with it so hard that clouds of black dust filled the air. With shouts of fury, the man retreated and stomped off, yelling promises of revenge.

James leant on the half-door of the signalbox and laughed until the tears streamed down his face.

"That'll teach the bully, won't it, Jack? I don't think he will report you. Otherwise he'll have to admit that you chased him away with a coal sack!"

The foreman must have said something, however, because soon there were official objections. "We can't have a mere animal operating such vital machinery! The passengers are protesting," said the Uitenhage station master. "What if there should be an accident?"

But there would be no accidents. Jack didn't make mistakes. James knew that or he wouldn't have trusted Jack the way he did.

However, James himself did make a mistake. One of the points had jammed. He hobbled his way over the rails to see what was wrong. A stone was caught in the gap. As James bent to take it out, his wooden peg-leg slipped on the gravel and he fell heavily, crushing his arm under him.

He lay there dazed, wondering if his arm was broken, and then became aware of a gentle hand stroking his face. It was Jack, whimpering as he pulled at James' body as if aware that it was dangerous to lie on the railway line.

"It's all right, Jack," he groaned. "I'm not dead. But I've hurt my arm badly. If the foreman finds out, he'll find a replacement for me at once and I'll lose my job for good. I've got to carry on. Jack, you'll have to do it for me until I'm better."

Jack nibbled gently at James' ear and appeared to understand. He helped his master to stand upright.

For the next three days, James lay on a mattress in a corner of the signalbox. At first he was in too much pain even to sit. Jack took over all his duties. He dashed out with the key when it was needed. He worked all the signal levers, even those for the distant signals. A little over a metre tall, he was strong enough to work the farthest signal about 1 200 metres away. Each evening he placed the trolley on the line, helped his master on to it and pushed him home to the little railway cottage. The next morning he brought him back to work.

On the fourth day a railway official in a smart blue coat glistening with gold braid appeared at the door. James was sitting on a stool but he was still unable to pull any of the levers.

"I have come to inform you that we have received a complaint," he said. As James started to explain about his injured arm, a train whistle blew in the distance, and Jack sprang into action, pulling exactly the correct signal levers. The official gaped as he watched. After the train had passed, there was a silence.

"I don't know what people are complaining about!" he muttered. "Seems to me that you and your...er...friend have everything completely under control. Well done!"

James smiled and smoothed down his heavy moustache. Of course there was no need for any alarm. Jack was the best friend he had ever had – and a darned good signalman as well!

It was the last time anyone complained. For nine years Jack gave the railway good and faithful service. The people who used the Uitenhage-Port Elizabeth line became very proud of their baboon signalman, but never so proud as James Edwin Wide himself.

BABOONS are often known by their Khoi name, Chacma. They live in troops all over southern Africa, provided there is food, water and either trees or rocks. Males can weigh as much as 44 kilograms and have a shoulder height of 80 centimetres. Because of their crop-raiding habits, we often forget the good baboons can do in the wild, particularly in controlling such insects as locusts. They have more intelligence than we sometimes are aware of. Eugene Marais, in his famous study *The Soul of the Ape,* found their mental processes so similar to ours that he could only compare chacma baboons to human standards.

JOCK OF THE BUSHVELD

Five of the bull terrier puppies were fat, strong, yellow little chaps with dark muzzles – just like their father. The sixth was a poor, miserable, little rat of a thing. He was a sort of dirty, pale half-and-half colour, and he had a dark, sharp, wizened little muzzle. That was Jock.

The other puppies would tumble over him and take his food. They would bump into him when he was stooping over the dish of milk and porridge, and his head was so big and his legs so weak that he would topple over and fall head over heels into the dish. His master was always picking him out of the food and scraping it off him.

One of the oxen, sniffing around the transport riders' camp, came up to examine the puppy. It moved towards him slowly, giving big sniffs at this strange, new object. The puppy stood quite still with his stumpy tail cocked and his head a little to one side. When the huge ox's nose was near him he gave a sudden, short bark. The ox nearly tumbled over with fright. Even when the great mountain of a thing gave a clumsy plunge and trotted off, the puppy's tail and ears flickered for a second, but they stiffened up again instantly. With another of those sharp, little barks, he took a couple of steps forward and cocked his head to the other side. That was Jock's way.

And that was why young Percy FitzPatrick, living a hard life in the bush in the days when Pilgrim's Rest was full of gold-diggers, chose Jock as his dog. He was trained to lie down, to stay on guard, and not to touch food until his master had told him to 'take it'. Jock learned to obey hand signals too. Sometimes he pressed up against his master when he was aiming his gun at something. FitzPatrick would look at Jock, and Jock knew quite well what that meant. Down would go his ears and he would back away, drop his stump of a tail, wag it feebly and open his mouth into a sort of foolish laugh that was his apology. As he grew, he looked less rat-like and more handsome, with a smooth golden-brown coat and a white patch on his chest.

Jock's first experience of hunting was on a hot day when his master had

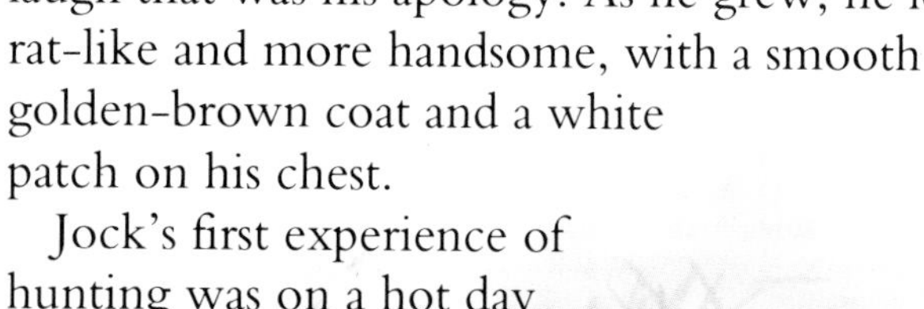

already shot at a steenbok and missed. As FitzPatrick sat in the shade of some thorn trees, a duiker stopped about 20 metres away. It was hardly possible to miss, so he aimed, fired and ran out after it, forgetting to take his gun with him.

Hit in the shoulder, the duiker stumbled, rolled over and over, then got up and dashed away on three legs. When he heard "After him, Jock," Jock was gone, taking a short cut to head it off. He caught up and jumped for its throat. The duiker, however, darted away, leaving him behind. By the time FitzPatrick caught up, Jock had a grip high on its back leg. Then the duiker fell, broke loose and thrust with its black spiky horns so swiftly that it seemed nothing could save Jock from being stabbed through and through. But if he could not catch the duiker, it would not catch him either.

On three legs, however, the duiker had no chance. In another minute Jock had it down again. FitzPatrick caught the struggling duiker by the head, held it down and tried to finish it with his knife. Neither man nor dog had learned yet what a buck can do with its hind legs. The supple body doubled up, and the hooves whizzed viciously by, striking the knife and sending it flying out of reach. With a sudden twist and a wrench, the duiker freed itself and was off again.

All this time Jock had been moving around, panting and licking his chops, longing to be at it again but not daring to join in without permission. When the duiker broke free, however, he waited for nothing and was on to it in one spring. He let go as it fell and, jumping free, had it by the throat before it could rise. Then it was his turn to learn the lesson of the duiker's feet.

The first kick went over his head and scraped harmlessly along his back. The second caught him on the shoulder, and the razor-like toe cut his side open as if it had been

Although Jock is often described as a Staffordshire terrier, his mother, Jess, was in fact a BULL TERRIER. A bull terrier is a sturdy, heavily-built, smooth-coated breed of dog, usually white but sometimes brown. A cross between terrier and bulldog, they were originally bred for bull-baiting in England, so they make excellent hunting dogs.

slashed with a knife. Then Jock showed his pluck and cleverness. He never flinched or loosened his grip for a second. He swung his body clear of the whizzing feet and tugged away vigorously, keeping the buck's neck stretched out. The kicks grew weaker, the duiker slackened, and Jock had won.

He was just as happy as a dog could be, and perhaps he was proud of the wound that left a straight line from his shoulder to his hip – a memento of his first real hunt.

Jock's favourite method of attack was tugging sideways so that a buck crossed its legs and came down immediately; then he had it by the throat before it could rise again. Only once did he make a dreadful mistake; and he paid for it – very nearly with his own life.

Jock was with FitzPatrick in a grove of bushy, wild plums when suddenly they stood face to face with a grand kudu bull less than a dozen metres away. Huge spiral horns and wide staring eyes – followed by a whirlwind of dust and leaves as it turned and fled. FitzPatrick fired hurriedly, and the great creature sank for a moment, almost to the ground. Then it struck up the slope, as FitzPatrick fired again and again – but each time a longer shot. He sent Jock on and followed as fast as he could.

FitzPatrick's old Martini rifle had one bad fault: it was always jamming. Unless the cartridges were kept well greased, the empty shells would stick. It jammed then, and all he could do was run on, towards Jock and the kudu.

The kudu's leg was broken, but his nimbleness was still astonishing. Knowing every trick of attack and defence, he was blazing with anger at this persistent little gadfly that worried him so and kept out of reach. He would back slowly, to tempt the dog on; then with a sudden lunge the great horns swished through the spot where Jock had been only a fraction of a second before.

Perhaps realising that attack from the front was useless, Jock went for the broken leg. He got a hold and dragged it back along the ground. The kudu tried to regain its footing, was tripped by its crossed legs and came down with a crash. As it fell, Jock shot around and fastened onto its nose. But this was no duiker, impala or rietbok. The kudu gave a snort of indignation and flung him off, sending him skidding along the ground.

Jock raced in again with head down and the little eyes black with fury. He was too mad to be wary and the long horns swung around with a swish. One black point seemed to pierce him through and through, showing clear out the other side, and a twist of the great head sent him twirling high up into the air. It had just missed him, passing under his stomach. He dropped with a thud, scrambled to his feet and raced in again.

Once more he fastened on the nose only to be shaken worse than before. The kudu literally flogged the ground with him. As FitzPatrick still wrestled with his rifle, he had to shut his eyes for it seemed as if the plucky dog would be beaten into pulp. Setting his foot against a tree, FitzPatrick wrenched until the empty cartridge flew out.

Reloading fast, he came around to within a metre of where Jock stood firm under the trunk of a tree, still hanging on to the kudu's nose. The hauling kudu seemed to stretch Jock's neck visibly. But the rifle shot was the end. As the splendid head dropped slowly over, Jock let go his hold.

He had not uttered a sound except the grunts that were knocked out of him.

Half-way between the Crocodile and Komati rivers, there are half a dozen small koppies with rich grasslands between. Where his master took cover by crawling, Jock felt the need to see what was ahead. As the grass was too high for him to see over, he took jumps of increasing strength. At the top of his jump his legs were all bunched up, his eyes staring eagerly and his ears flapped out giving him a look of comic astonishment.

That was how he spotted the string of kudu. FitzPatrick got in one shot before they cantered away. The last of the troop, a big cow, stumbled but cantered on. By then, Jock was close behind. He may have thought there was a broken leg to grip – or perhaps he was just too bold. Anyway, he jumped at one of the hind legs, and at the same moment the kudu lashed out viciously. One foot struck him under the jaw close to the throat, whipped his head back, and sent him spinning through the air.

He lay limp and motionless, with blood oozing from his mouth and nose. FitzPatrick felt desperately for his heart-beat and called, "Jock!" again and again. Remembering a nearby pool, he filled his hat with water and poured it over the limp dog. He dribbled water into Jock's mouth, as he pressed the dog's sides to try and restore his breathing.

The old hat was leaky, and FitzPatrick was returning for a second hatful when he saw Jock roll over, his head shaking in a dazed manner and his eyes blinking. At the touch of a hand, his ears moved up and the stumpy tail scraped feebly in the dead leaves. He took no notice when FitzPatrick called his name, for he was stone deaf. From that day on, he depended on signals, for he never heard another sound. This deafness didn't seem to worry him in the veld, but it became dangerous for Jock in camp. He would take a snooze on the warm earth of the track and several times was nearly run over by a wagon. Meanwhile, to earn his living, Percy FitzPatrick was forced to make long treks to Mozambique. For a while he left Jock in the care of an old friend, Tom Barnett, who kept a trader's store. FitzPatrick never saw his dog again.

One bright, moonlit night, Tom was aroused by a clatter of falling boxes and the wild cries of his chickens in the fenced-off yard. He grabbed his rifle, opened the little window which gave him a view of the chicken house and waited for the thief to appear. Then the dim form of a dog appeared in the doorway. Tom lifted the gun slowly and took careful aim.

When the smoke cleared away, the figure of the dog lay still. Tom went back to bed, satisfied.

In the morning, Tom pushed open the reed gate and made his way towards the chicken house. Under the porch where the sunlight touched it, something shone like polished gold.

Jock lay stretched out on his side – he might have been asleep. But on the snow-white chest there was one red spot. And inside the chicken house lay the thieving mongrel dog – dead. Jock had done his duty.

HUBERTA THE HIPPO

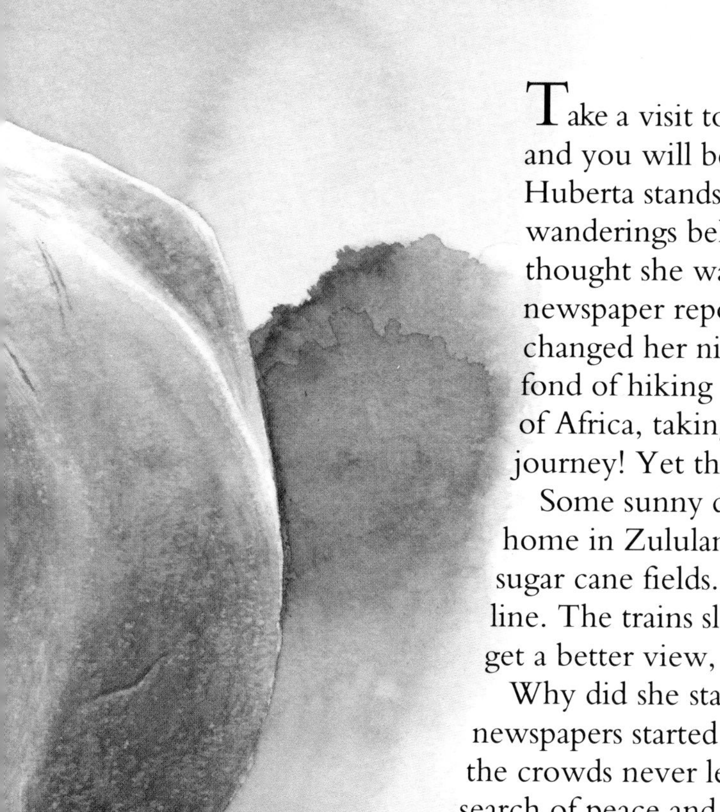

Take a visit to the Kaffrarian Museum in King William's Town and you will be able to view the heaviest heroine of all time! Huberta stands firmly among the other large mammals, her wanderings behind her now. (At the start of her travels, people thought she was male. 'Hubert the Hippo' said the first newspaper reports, until somebody realised that was wrong and changed her nickname to Huberta.) Groups of hikers today are fond of hiking trails. To cover 1 600 kilometres along the coast of Africa, taking nearly three years over it, would be quite a journey! Yet that is what Huberta did – all by herself.

Some sunny day in November 1928, Huberta left her lagoon home in Zululand and started to munch her way through the sugar cane fields. For a while, she lived in a pool near the railway line. The trains slowed down as they passed so that everyone could get a better view, and passengers even threw fruit to her.

Why did she start her travels? Nobody knows. But once the newspapers started writing about her, she became famous. After that the crowds never left her alone. So she probably kept on the move in search of peace and quiet.

On a warm January evening in 1929, a garage-owner was driving home near Tongaat when he found a narrow bridge blocked by a large animal. Huberta, disturbed by the glaring headlights, stared at the car and then decided she didn't like it. She walked haughtily away and then headed towards the nearest lagoon.

Natal had a new tourist attraction! People hired buses and crashed their way through the bushes to catch a glimpse of Huberta. Several took one look at her huge tusks and cavernous mouth and retreated hastily. She was, after all, a wild animal. For a month she stayed in the cool waters of the Umhlanga Lagoon. Then she went travelling again and arrived in Durban.

The Durban Country Club, with its golf course alongside, was a place for well-dressed diners and polite conversation as a rule. But the rules were broken on the last night of March when Huberta peered through the main gate. The Club steward saw her and reported it. Shrieks and squeals of excitement brought everyone running. Huberta retreated fast towards the tenth hole. The humans followed. Gentlemen in bow ties and dinner jackets, ladies in long dresses and high-heeled shoes, waiters in crisp uniforms – all went charging over the golf course after the frightened hippo. Sensibly, she hid in some bushes. Her pursuers got bored with searching and went back to the Club for a last drink.

It was still dark the following morning – April 1st – when she reappeared in the middle of Durban. A wide-eyed ricksha-puller discovered her huge hippopotamus bulk, lit up red, green and blue from the neon lights, outside the West Street Pharmacy. It was the most impressive April Fool's Day joke he had ever seen! But Huberta was far too large and real. He swung his feathered bicycle-carriage around and fled.

Concrete and tarmac was no home for a hippo, however. When early morning crowds started to gather where Huberta stood solidly across the tramlines outside the Federal Hotel, she beat a retreat through Victoria Park. From there, she was glad to find her way back to the Umgeni River mouth and submerge herself in its cool waters.

After that, the hunt was on in earnest. Reporters wanted to catch the latest story, photographers wanted to catch her on film, zoo-keepers wanted to catch her. The Natal provincial council also reminded the public that hippos were 'royal game', and could not be shot or captured without a special permit. So Huberta was protected even by the law.

As she fled from river to river, moving along the Natal south coast towards Transkei, she was greeted with more than mere popularity. The Zulus wondered if she was in some way connected with the spirit of Shaka. Near Bendigo, the Indians declared her 'the Protector of the Poor'. *The Star* reported how "Sacrificial fires were lighted and peace offerings made to Huberta". On the Wild Coast, the Pondos were worried that she might represent the spirit of a famous sangoma, so they dared not stop her munching through their maize fields.

By now Huberta had gained world fame. A poem about the persecuted hippo appeared in the London magazine *Punch*. Newspapers in England, America, India, Egypt and Australia carried details of her travels. It was happily predicted that she would arrive in Cape Town in time for Christmas.

By March 1930, she had reached the pretty village of Port St Johns and decided to stay. For six months she wallowed happily in the river and feasted in the gardens on either side. Though the river's name, Mzimvubu, means 'home of the hippos', no hippopotamus had been seen there in living memory. But Huberta was quite content in her new home.

When the weather became warmer, Huberta moved again – past the rocky headlands of the Wild Coast towards the farming country around East London. By day she hid in the river valleys, by night she selected choice plants and vegetables from farms and gardens. Huberta's fate was argued out in the newspaper columns. Farmers threatened to shoot her if she broke any more fences and ate their crops. Letters begged the authorities to capture Huberta for her own safety, for several zoos were eager to secure such a famous resident. Other letters deplored the idea that such a free, roaming animal should be confined to a cage. As more attempts were made to catch her, so Huberta was continually forced to move on.

There was even a report that, exhausted by her travels, she went to sleep on the railway line near East London. The engine driver blew his whistle loudly, and as Huberta failed to wake, gave her a gentle nudge with the 'cow-catcher' front of the engine. She snorted her protests, rose indignantly to her feet and lumbered away. That, at least, was the story the engine driver told the newspapers!

In April 1931, the poor tired hippopotamus was taking refuge in the Keiskamma River near Peddie. There, a farmer's son saw the tracks of a large animal in his garden. With his father and brother, he followed the spoor and spotted some creature in the river spouting water through its nostrils. The three of them opened fire and shot every time it rose to the surface. Bleeding badly but still alive, Huberta moved away. The next morning, the farmer found her again and fired twice with his rifle. That ended her suffering.

A HIPPOPOTAMUS (the word means 'river horse') can weigh as much as 1 500 kilograms and stands approximately 1,5 metres at the shoulder. A hippo needs to live in water, otherwise its skin will dry out. However, hippos seldom stay submerged for more than two or three minutes at a time. They are active at night, resting during the day. They usually stay within or around their chosen territory, which they defend vigorously if they have young calves. Their huge jaws are quite able to bite a crocodile in half!

2507

THE FAMOUS SOMERSET

This is almost more of a detective story than an animal story, but that makes it all the more exciting. There was a horse called Somerset and he *was* famous – exactly what for you must decide yourself.

George Jameson, a successful Durban businessman, was deeply in love with Pauline. She loved him too, and particularly adored his skill in storytelling. He told pioneering tales of his father Charles Jameson who had trekked up the Drakensberg in 1838, and stirring adventures of his father's friend Jan Hofmeyr, but above all she liked most the story of the horse Somerset. So who is to blame George if he embroidered the story a little? All good stories grow in the telling!

He told how, when Jan Hofmeyr was preparing to join the Great Trek, he knew that he needed a strong, sturdy horse. So he exchanged his farm land, which he was leaving behind, for cattle and a good hunter. "Steady as a rock, old boy," declared the retired English officer whose horse it was. "You won't find a better horse anywhere. Trained in the military riding school. He's called Somerset – after our Governor, Lord Charles Somerset."

Though Jan had no love for the British Governor, he examined the bay horse and agreed it was a fine animal. Standing fifteen hands high, Somerset had a small head like an Arab's, a satin smooth coat like a cloth of gold. He had a flowing black mane and dark stripes on his forequarters.

The other Boers on trek admired the horse too. He was as mild-mannered as any pet, yet fast enough to run down an ostrich and trained to ignore gunfire. So when Jan found himself inside the Boer laager at the Battle of Blood River, he was proud to lend Somerset to their commandant, Andries Pretorius. After the Zulus had made countless attacks and failed to penetrate the gun-defended laager, it was on Somerset that Pretorius galloped out at the head of his few hundred horsemen. They met determined resistance from the Zulu warriors, but after three sorties they turned the victory into an overwhelming defeat.

"You should have seen him, my darling!" said George, making most of it up as he went along. "His eyes full of fire, his girth deep, his forelegs straight! As I saw Pretorius gallop out, elephant gun in hand, coatless, sjambok on his wrist and bending over Somerset's neck, I knew there was never a smarter soldier."

With Dingaan's army scattered, the Boers began to settle on the land they had won. But when the British reoccupied Natal in 1842, Andries Pretorius gathered the Boer commandos to drive them out and Jan once again lent him the horse Somerset. The Boers camped at Congella, besieging the British troops in the fort. Many eyes admired the fine bay horse. So it was hardly surprising that one dark night a Griqua crept into the Boer laager and, pretending he was a servant, quietly untied the rein and led Somerset away into the British camp where they gladly bought the horse from him.

The British, desperately short of supplies, needed to send a message asking for relief. It was Dick King who volunteered to make the ride. And it was here that George's storytelling ran away with him. According to the story he told Pauline, Dick King rode Somerset all the way to Grahamstown, both of them arriving exhausted.

"What became of Somerset?" asked Pauline.

George replied, "The news in the military barracks the next morning was that King lay in the hospital and Somerset was dead."

It made a great ending to a good story – and that's the way that it has gone into the history books. However, George Jameson wasn't there with Dick King, and someone else was. Dick himself never spoke about his famous ride in later years, but the Zulu who rode with him part of the way did record his memories. Ndongeni twice dictated his version of what had happened.

He remembered clearly how they "started off at midnight, King riding a white horse and I a bay one." Now, Somerset was not a white horse! As a good detective, what can you deduce from the

clues? Surely, that if Somerset did indeed take part in that famous ride, it was Ndongeni who rode him and not Dick King!

So let's leave George telling tall stories to his adoring Pauline and find out what really happened to the famous Somerset.

Dick King was certainly the best man in the British camp to attempt to get the vital message through. Four years before, when news reached the English at Port Natal of a threatened Zulu attack on the Boer trekkers, Dick had set off on foot and covered the 192 kilometres in four days and four nights. He arrived just too late to save Retief's camp, but he walked on a further 16 kilometres and reached Gerrit Maritz in time to help him form a laager and defend it.

On the night of 25 May 1842, the Cato brothers helped King and Ndongeni cross Durban Bay in a rowing boat with two army horses swimming behind – one of which could well have been Somerset. King mounted the white horse and Ndongeni was on the bay riding a saddle without stirrups. They rode through the night to avoid being seen. They crossed rivers close to the sea, because they feared the Boers might be guarding the normal river crossings further inland. Dick King swam across each river in his shirt, while Ndongeni (who could not swim) kept King's clothes and clutched his horse's mane. Ndongeni remembered how his bay horse "was very frisky, and inclined to leap where less powerful animals would only walk or wade". That certainly sounds like the Somerset we have come to know.

LORD CHARLES SOMERSET, Governor of the Cape between 1814 and 1817 after whom Dick King's famous horse was named, was a keen importer of thoroughbred horses to the Cape.

A true thoroughbred is descended from one of three particular Arab sires and 50 chosen English mares. As the horse, Somerset, is described as having had an Arab head, it is quite possible that he might even have been bred from the horses brought to the Cape colony by his namesake, Lord Charles.

At a British military camp by the Umgazi mouth, Ndongeni was provided with stirrups and a fresh horse. His legs, however, had become so sore that a few days later he had to turn back. Dick went on alone. He knew the mission stations ahead (having been a wagon driver over that area for many years) and planned to call there, as he knew that one horse could not go all the way. We know that he changed horses at Buntingville and then again at Butterworth. So he certainly did not cruelly ride one horse to death. He did, however, get through to Grahamstown only ten days after leaving Port Natal, having covered about 960 kilometres. Soon he was on his way back, travelling with relief troops and supplies, and fully deserves his fame as 'saviour of Natal'. Ndongeni was on the shore watching his master's triumphant return.

So what happened to Somerset? If he was one of the horses supplied at the start of the ride, then he must have been replaced at the Umgazi mouth. Duly rested, as an army horse he would have been returned to Port Natal, and there appears to be evidence that he ended his days on King's sugarcane farm at Isipingo. We shall never know for sure – but it seems a kinder fate for 'the famous Somerset'.

SMURF AND HENRY

"Save Smurf and Henry!" *The Cape Times* was the first to print the story. Soon United Press International, *Die Burger*, the *Daily Telegraph* in London, and even the American Broadcasting Corporation from Detroit were scrambling to cover the pathetic tale of two lovers about to be parted by heartless officials. All the stranger, because the lovebirds were just that – a penguin and a pelican!

The young jackass penguin had been starving and sick with enteritis when Walter Mangold first saw him. Without proper treatment, the bird was going to die. So the penguin, soon named Smurf, was nursed back to health and made its home in Walter's bird sanctuary, the World of Birds. Smurf enjoyed his new life and quickly learned to parade for meals outside the kitchen at precisely the right time each day.

Henry should actually have been called Henrietta as she was female. She had been brought to the park with a badly broken wing and was one of hundreds of birds treated and cared for by Walter Mangold and his team. Unable to fly, the pelican adapted happily to life on ground level – and there she met Smurf. Quite simply, they 'fell in love'.

From then on, visitors to the World of Birds delighted in watching them. Henry would wrap her long bill round Smurf's tubby body and stand happily as cameras clicked at close range. They had another pose too: with Smurf's head actually inside the pelican's large beak. The birds were completely tame and accepted humans without complaint, even when Henry was referred to as a 'perlemoen' instead of a pelican! When Henry wandered away with her long, slow, well-measured steps, Smurf would try desperately to keep up. His staggering waddle made him look almost drunk.

The World of Birds wildlife sanctuary nestles in the steep-sided green valley of Hout Bay on the Cape Peninsula. All the correct permits are applied for to keep their vast collection of over three thousand birds, as well as smaller animals like bushbabies, monkeys and tortoises. Penguins, however, need special permission. So Walter Mangold was horrified to receive a letter from the Department of Nature Conservation.

"I regret to inform you", said the letter, "that your application to keep two jackass penguins in captivity was not successful. The alarming decline in the number of penguins along our coast has resulted in a departmental policy decision not to allow healthy penguins to be kept in captivity and they must, therefore, be rehabilitated and returned to the sea. Under the circumstances you are advised to contact SANCCOB to collect the birds before 15 January 1981 in order to rehabilitate the birds and release them".

The letter arrived on a Friday afternoon. That left only three days in which to do anything. One of the penguins was duly returned to its natural environment, but surely not Smurf? Smurf was tame – he had lost his ability to survive in the sea. To return him to such an unfamiliar life would be an act of cruelty, not compassion. Walter Mangold didn't know what to do.

Then *The Cape Times* heard of the story. They printed the details on Monday and, within a day, both the World of Birds and the Department of Nature Conservation had received countless indignant telephone calls. Wisely, Walter phoned the government department and spoke to the Deputy Director. Such problems are always best handled personally. They both agreed that the matter was getting out of hand.

The Deputy Director promised to pay an official visit to examine the merits of this special case. His shiny car duly drew up outside the World of Birds. The important official walked slowly up the

twisting paths, where bright parrots screamed from their perches, and through the large walk-through aviaries. He seemed increasingly impressed by what he saw. Walter was beside him, his heart pounding. Would the required permission be given or not?

Finally they encountered the ill-fated pair – Smurf and Henry, who were not at all flustered by their important visitor. They just wanted to stay friends and stay together – and the Deputy Director smiled and agreed that they should.

The news was flashed round the world by television, radio and newspapers. "Official: Smurf and Henry can live together." The contented birds filled the prime spot on the evening news. Even more visitors flocked to the World of Birds to see the remarkable pair. Henry played with her ball and gulped down whole pilchards. Smurf waddled quite happily alongside.

The WHITE PELICAN is a large bird with a pouch under its long beak, and lives in flocks along the south-western coast and off Natal. During the breeding season its white feathers take on a pinkish colour. They hatch their chalky white eggs on the ground in untidy nests made of seaweed and feathers.

The JACKASS PENGUIN gets its name from its cry which sounds like the braying of a donkey. Black-backed with a dark line down each side of its white chest, the jackass penguin usually breeds in colonies on coastal islands, digging burrows in the hard sand or among rocky boulders. Penguin nests are often lined with old feathers and dry seaweed.

In the springtime, Henry (or Henrietta) was transformed from a blushing teenager to a desirable young lady as her plumage made the normal changes of her breed. The skin on her face and bill shone a waxy off-white, touched in places with a peachy pink. She clamoured for the attention of the bird handlers and especially of Smurf.

The love story could have ended there. But 'the eternal love triangle' can occur, even with birds! A few months later, a rare white jackass penguin was found on a False Bay beach. She was clogged with oil and moulting badly. Restored to health at the World of Birds, the white penguin wandered around and soon met and fell in love with Smurf. Henry didn't really mind and even played with the newcomer. Then Smurf seemed to decide that his previous 'mixed marriage' might not work out, so he started paying more attention to his new companion. Luckily, a very handsome male pelican arrived at the sanctuary with an injured wing and stole Henry's heart.

So Henry and Smurf parted as friends, and today they still see each other from time to time.

THE FISH WITH FOUR LEGS

"You know I don't want to be interrupted. I have all these university exam papers to mark." Professor JLB Smith of the chemistry department at Rhodes University was understandably annoyed. But the bulky packet that had arrived by post caught his interest.

It had been sent to him by the director of the East London Museum, Miss Marjorie Courtenay-Latimer. A keen student of matters relating to fish, Prof Smith had often helped out at the museum. Now his friend had sent him drawings of a strange fish she had seen amongst the catch of a trawler in East London. It was a large fish, over a metre in length, of a strange purple-blue colour. Could he help identify it? she asked. He examined her drawings with amazement. They were like no fish that he had ever seen before!

But the exam papers still had to be marked, so it was six weeks before Prof Smith could visit East London to see the fish for himself. By then, it had been stuffed and mounted, and its soft insides thrown away. Its blue scales had turned a shiny brown from the preservation process and four stubby fins stuck out from its heavy body, almost like stunted legs. He stared at it, compared notes from books on prehistoric creatures and eventually looked at Miss Courtenay-Latimer, amazed.

"This fish ceased to exist millions of years ago – or so we all believed. It is a coelacanth. It has to be. A live coelacanth!" Prof Smith beamed with delight. "At least, it was alive when it was caught. Oh, what a pity you couldn't preserve its insides so we could know what it ate and how it lived."

Scientists all over the world were astounded when the discovery of the coelacanth was made public. The story of 'the living fossil' appeared in newspapers, and everyone asked the same question: were there more? Prof Smith asked fishermen along South Africa's eastern ports to watch out for the strange fish. Nobody found one.

The next year, 1939, the Second World War started and newspapers had grimmer stories to print than vague hopes of catching prehistoric fish. But Prof Smith hadn't forgotten. Some scientists guessed that as the coelacanth hadn't been seen or caught before, it must live in deep waters. Prof Smith studied the coelacanth very carefully and disagreed with them. It looked far more like a shallow-water fish. Where could it have come from? He decided it might have come from the coast of East Africa or Madagascar.

In 1950, he tried to organise an official fishing expedition to search for coelacanth in the tropical Indian Ocean but his plans were not accepted. So he and his wife went on expeditions of their own. He had leaflets printed in English, French and Portuguese, with a picture of the coelacanth, offering £100 reward. A fair sum in those days!

Towards the end of 1952, Prof Smith had only been home a few hours after his latest expedition when a telegram arrived from a Captain Hunt. He sailed a fishing schooner and had been interested to hear of Smith's search. His crew had caught a large fish off the Comores, a group of islands between Madagascar and Mozambique, and he was convinced it was a coelacanth.

How could Smith get there? There was no air service. A boat would take weeks. By the time he arrived, the body of the fish may have rotted and those important internal organs would be lost again, and he would have to start his search all over again.

In vain, Prof Smith tried to find some way of flying to the Comores. But it was the Christmas holidays and nobody seemed very interested in his search for a fish which was thought to be extinct for thousands of years. He contacted everyone he could think of and even phoned important government ministers. But he met with no success. People were either too busy enjoying their

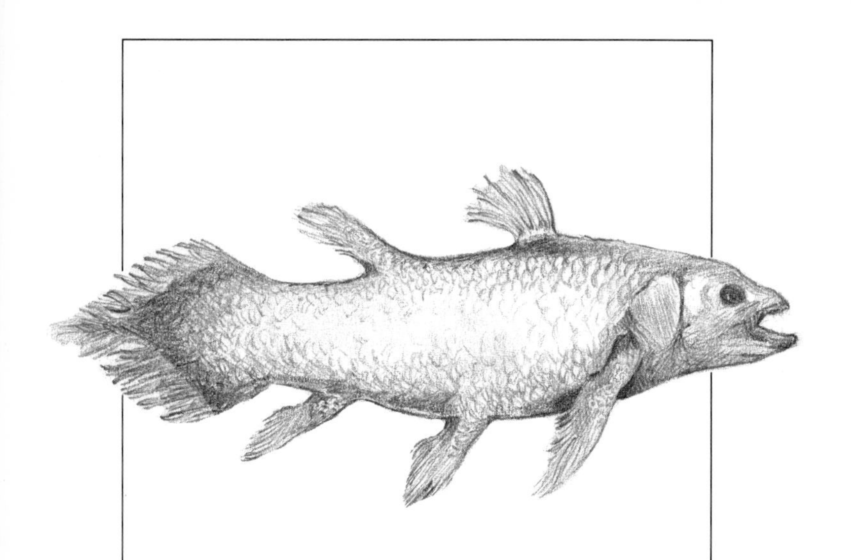

The COELACANTH is a large fish which was quite common about 250 million years ago. Fossils of this fish have been found, and it was thought to have become extinct 60 million years ago. Its Latin name is *Latimeria chalumnae* in honour of a past director of the East London museum, Miss Marjorie Courtenay-Latimer, who first noted its appearance in modern times. Attention has recently been focused on diving expeditions in South African waters, where it is predicted that coelacanth are living at deep levels.

holiday or simply not interested. Eventually, quite late in the evening, he phoned the Prime Minister himself. Dr DF Malan was on holiday at his seaside house in the Strand, and he was already in bed. His wife took the call but refused to disturb him and said she would tell him in the morning. Prof Smith put the phone down and, without much hope, sat back with a cup of tea.

However, Dr Malan had heard the telephone ring and he insisted his wife tell him about the matter. He knew of the professor and by luck Smith's book, *Sea Fishes of Southern Africa*, was in the house. The Prime Minister read the section on the coelacanth carefully. Then he said, "The man that wrote this book would not ask my help at a time like this unless it was desperately important. I must speak to him".

So, despite his wife's protests, Dr Malan phoned Smith at 10.30 pm that same night. Prof Smith explained urgently the significance of the coelacanth catch and the need to reach the Comores as soon as possible. This was a matter of importance to the world and South African pride was at stake.

The voice through the phone said, "I must congratulate you on your Afrikaans. It is excellent".

There was a long pause while Prof Smith sat and hoped. Then the Prime Minister told him that he would arrange for a military plane first thing in the morning.

So, a dazed Prof Smith reached the Comores in a military Dakota, where the captain who had sent the telegram met him with the words. "Don't worry, it's a coelacanth all right!" And it was.

A large coffin-like box was opened and at first all Smith could see was a mass of cotton wool. Suppose they were wrong? Suppose he had flown all this way on a false alarm? Then as they uncovered the fish, he saw the bony head, the large purple-blue scales, the spiny fins. Prof Smith found tears splashing on his hands as he knelt beside the box and realised that he was crying.

There, in front of him, was a creature as rare as a dinosaur – a fish which had survived unchanged since the days of the dinosaurs. As the newspapers had called it, those years before, 'a living fossil'.

Prof Smith had discovered the home of the coelacanths. Since then, several more of these strange 'four-legged' fish have been caught off the Comores. The local fishermen don't find that strange at all. They've been catching coelacanths for hundreds of years!

AUTHOR'S ACKNOWLEDGEMENTS

I would like to extend my warmest thanks to everyone who helped to make this book possible: Roelf Attwell and the Wallers family of Betty's Bay; Walter Mangold; Susan Fowkes; Nick Carter; Marty Das; Dr EG Nisbet (University of Saskatchewan, Canada); Paul du Toit; Peter Slingsby; Peter Norton (Department of Nature Conservation, Kimberley); Joyce Scallan; the Simonstown Naval Museum.

References used include:

'Coelacanth' – The fish that came back from the dead (R Auerbach); *Dick King, Feats Fame Family* (J Scallan); *Dick King, Saviour of Natal* (C Eyre); *Discovering Southern Africa* (TV Bulpin); *Huberta the Wandering Hippo* (DA Webb); *Huberta's Journey* (C van Straten); *Illustrated Guide to Southern Africa* (TV Bulpin); *Jack the Signalman Baboon* (FW FitzSimons); *Jock of the Bushveld* (P FitzPatrick); *Just Nuisance* and *Just Nuisance Carries On* (LM Steyn); *Just Nuisance, AB* (T Sisson); *Old Fourlegs* (Prof JLB Smith); *The Elephants of Knysna (N Carter); They Came from the Sea* (M Rowe); *They Made This Land* (J Heale); World of Birds newsletters.

Struik Timmins Publishers
(a member of The Struik Publishing Group (Pty) Ltd)
Cornelis Struik House
80 McKenzie Street
Cape Town
8001

Reg. No.: 54/00965/07

First published 1991
Second impression 1993

Editor Sean Fraser
Design and cover design Robert Meas
Illustrations Lorreta Chegwidden and Graeme Chegwidden 1991

Typesetting by Struik DTP
Reproduction by Unifoto (Pty) Ltd, Cape Town
Printed and bound by South China Printing Co., Hong Kong

ISBN 0 86978 553 2